50

Biblical Affirmations for a Fearless Pregnancy

By Elizabeth Jimenez
Author and Creator of MamaFearless.com

Dear Reader,

Congratulations on your pregnancy! It is my most heartfelt prayer that you find a place of confidence, capability and excitement regarding your pregnancy, labor and childbirth experience.

Mama Fearless is dedicated to helping you achieve, conquer and thrive during your pregnancy, regardless of your method or the challenges you face.

In this book, you will find 50 affirmations and scriptures to help you build your confidence and strength. Pregnancy is not without its challenges, but that doesn't mean we can't persevere and achieve a fulfilling childbirth with fond memories.

I want you all to know that I salute you, admire you and support you through your journey. You have been entrusted with the precious gift of life—the most beautiful miracle of mothers.

May God Bless and Keep You,

Elizabeth

ONE

My Body Is Capable

Every part of my body is given to the task of carrying my baby— from my muscles, to my bones, to my bloodstream and my organs. Miraculous things are taking place inside of me to physically accommodate a baby. My body is completely focused on the task at hand.

My body is capable of labor. My body is capable of contracting, relaxing, and delivering my baby. My body is naturally capable, created capable.

I may sometimes feel incapable. When I feel incapable, that doesn't mean that what I feel is true. That doesn't change how capable I really am.

My Body Is Capable

HABAKKUK 3:19

"The Lord God is my strength, and he will make my feet like hinds' feet, and he will make me to walk upon mine high places..."

Notes:_____

_____

_____

_____

_____

_____

_____

_____

_____

_____

_____

_____

_____

_____

_____

_____

_____

_____

_____

_____

_____

_____

_____

TWO

I Am Mentally Capable of Making Choices for Myself

I can make choices. My mind is clear and focused, and I am using that mental focus to choose the steps I take during my pregnancy. I feel mentally strong and sure.

While I may be tired and emotional, I can find a place in prayer to renew my mind. The decisions I make for my body and my pregnancy are confident and determined. I will choose what's best. I will pay attention to what my body needs, and I will make the right decisions to supply those needs.

I may not always get it right. I may stumble in my mental focus. When that happens, I will learn from that and keep pressing on. My mistakes will not cause me to doubt my mental abilities.

I Am Mentally Capable

ROMANS 12:2

"And be not conformed to this world: but be ye transformed by the renewing of your mind, that ye may prove what is that good, and acceptable, and perfect, will of God."

Notes:_____

_____
_____
_____
_____
_____
_____
_____
_____
_____
_____
_____
_____
_____
_____
_____
_____
_____
_____
_____
_____
_____
_____
_____

THREE

I Have Peace Against Self-Doubt

Because I am mentally capable, I have peace against self-doubt. I know that self-doubt will come, and when it does, I will be ready for it. Self-doubt will not win. I have peace that I can make decisions. I have peace that I can learn and grow.

I have peace that I can carry my baby and make the right choices. I have peace that I will conquer and thrive during my pregnancy, even when I feel insecure at times. I have peace that I can find a place of confidence in my abilities, in my body, and in my mind.

I have peace in my mind.

PHILIPPIANS 4:7

"And the peace of God, which passeth all understanding, shall keep your hearts and minds through Christ Jesus."

Notes:_____

_____

_____

_____

_____

_____

_____

_____

_____

_____

_____

_____

_____

_____

_____

_____

_____

_____

_____

_____

_____

_____

FOUR

I Have Strength In My Mind

Because I have peace, I now have room for strength. My mind is strong. I can make a choice and stand by it, even when I feel insecure. Everything about my mind is centered on my baby. That makes me the ultimate decision-maker. I have strength in my mind to fight against self-doubt and fear.

I have the strength of mind to control my thoughts. When I don't feel mentally strong, I know that it will not last. The changes of pregnancy can cause me to sometimes feel unstable, but I will fight this off. I know I have strength of mind, and I will hold fast. I will exercise that strength and do what I can to maintain it.

I have strength in my mind.

2 CORINTHIANS 10:5

"Casting down imaginations, and every high thing that exalteth itself against the knowledge of God, and bringing into captivity every thought to the obedience of Christ."

Notes:_____

_____

_____

_____

_____

_____

_____

_____

_____

_____

_____

_____

_____

_____

_____

_____

_____

_____

_____

_____

_____

_____

FIVE

I Love My Pregnancy

I love my pregnancy. Not everything about my pregnancy is easy, but I love that I am carrying my baby, that I have this wonderful opportunity. I am so thankful that the Lord entrusted me with this treasure, and I know the love I feel will last forever.

The love I feel now is like no other. This love will carry on, even after my baby is born, and will only grow stronger.

When I have hard days, painful days, or tired days, I may not feel well but I still love my pregnancy, because I know what it will bring.

I love my pregnancy

ISAIAH 49:15

"Can a woman forget her sucking child, that she should not have compassion on the son of her womb? yea, they may forget, yet will I not forget thee."

Notes:_____

_____

_____

_____

_____

_____

_____

_____

_____

_____

_____

_____

_____

_____

_____

_____

_____

_____

_____

_____

_____

_____

_____

_____

_____

_____

SIX

My Baby Is Strong

My baby kicks and moves. My baby is sometimes quiet and restful. My baby's movements are an everyday reminder that they are strong, developing, growing.

I sometimes feel fear and worry about my baby. I sometimes worry when my baby doesn't move for a little while. But I understand that all of this—the movement, the stillness, is part of the growth of my baby.

Each day brings new development and growth for my baby. The miraculous transformations that occur everyday are incredible! I am so proud of my baby, and I cannot wait to hold my baby in my arms.

My baby is strong.

JEREMIAH 29:11

*"For I know the thoughts that I
think toward you, saith the Lord,
thoughts of peace, and not of evil,
to give you an expected end."*

Notes:_____

_____

_____

_____

_____

_____

_____

_____

_____

_____

_____

_____

_____

_____

_____

_____

_____

_____

_____

_____

_____

_____

_____

SEVEN

I Am Not Afraid of Pregnancy

I am not afraid of being pregnant. I am unsure, even worried at times—but I am not afraid. I was created to handle pregnancy. I don't understand everything but that does not make afraid.

There are times when I may feel fear. Feeling fear can come and go. It doesn't have to control me. It doesn't make me afraid of being pregnant. I look forward to each day of pregnancy, because each day a new miracle is taking place within my body.

When I begin to feel afraid, I remind myself that I have love instead, and it drives my fear away.

I am not afraid of pregnancy.

1 JOHN 4:18

"There is no fear in love; but perfect love casteth out fear: because fear hath torment. He that feareth is not made perfect in love."

Notes:_____

_____

_____

_____

_____

_____

_____

_____

_____

_____

_____

_____

_____

_____

_____

_____

_____

_____

_____

_____

_____

_____

_____

_____

_____

EIGHT

I Place My Pregnancy In God's Hands

There are times when I may feel doubt and weariness. There are times when I may battle fear and insecurity. But I place my pregnancy in God's hands.

I will do my part and I will work hard for my baby and my pregnancy. There is surety and safety when I know He holds my life and my circumstances in His hands. I find immeasurable peace in that.

I may sometimes forget and grow anxious, putting my burdens back on my own shoulders. But I can be reminded to place my pregnancy back in His hands, and I feel comfort once again.

I place my pregnancy in God's hands.

1 PETER 5:7

"Casting all your care upon him;
for he careth for you."

Notes:_____

_____

_____

_____

_____

_____

_____

_____

_____

_____

_____

_____

_____

_____

_____

_____

_____

_____

_____

_____

_____

_____

_____

NINE

My Body Is Adaptable

My body is adaptable to the changes of pregnancy. My body is moving and changing, ever making room for my little one. I can feel the changes, day by day. It's part of the deep connection between my little one and me.

As my baby grows, I grow, too—in body, in mind and in love. My body can accommodate and hold my baby, protect my baby, and nourish my baby.

My body is adaptable.

PSALM 100:3

"Know ye that the Lord he is God: it is he that hath made us, and not we ourselves; we are his people, and the sheep of his pasture."

Notes:_____

_____

_____

_____

_____

_____

_____

_____

_____

_____

_____

_____

_____

_____

_____

_____

_____

_____

_____

_____

_____

_____

_____

TEN

My Mind Is Capable of Making Choices for My Baby

My mind is strong. My mind is focused. I can make decisions for myself, but I can also make decisions for my baby. No one knows my baby like I do. I am the one person who can make the most instinctive choice for the well-being of my little one.

I may hear many different opinions. I may feel many different pressures. The choice is up to me, and I can have confidence that I am perfectly capable of making the best choice to bring my baby into the world.

My mind is capable of making choices for my baby.

COLOSSIANS 3:2

*"Set your affection on things above,
not on things on the earth."*

Notes:_____

_____

_____

_____

_____

_____

_____

_____

_____

_____

_____

_____

_____

_____

_____

_____

_____

_____

_____

_____

_____

_____

_____

_____

ELEVEN

My Body Is Fearfully & Wonderfully Made

My body is beautifully made. I've been created with the most perfect care. Nothing about my body is an accident. I have everything it takes to carry my baby, and when the time comes, I have everything it takes to labor. I have everything it takes to deliver my baby.

My body is not a lemon. Whatever physical challenges I face only make me more determined to become stronger. I am everything my baby needs.

My body is fearfully and wonderfully made.

PSALM 139:14

"I will praise thee; for I am fearfully and wonderfully made: marvellous are thy works; and that my soul knoweth right well."

Notes:_____

_____

_____

_____

_____

_____

_____

_____

_____

_____

_____

_____

_____

_____

_____

_____

_____

_____

_____

_____

_____

_____

TWEVLE

My Mind Is Completely In
Tune With My Baby

My mind is keen and aware. I may feel tired, but I am completely in tune with my baby. My thoughts are focused on my little one. We are connected in a deep way. It cannot be explained, but it doesn't need to be. This connection is precious, something between the two of us that is a gift from God.

I feel it every day, and I make my decisions based on that connection. This special connection is growing steadily and will be present between us for our entire lifetime.

My mind is perfectly in tune with my baby.

JEREMIAH 33:2-3

"Thus saith the Lord the maker thereof, the Lord that formed it, to establish it; the Lord is his name; Call unto me, and I will answer thee, and show thee great and mighty things, which thou knowest not."

Notes:_____

_____

_____

_____

_____

_____

_____

_____

_____

_____

_____

_____

_____

_____

_____

_____

_____

_____

_____

_____

_____

_____

_____

_____

_____

THIRTEEN

I Find Peace In The Midst of Stress

The world around me is busy and changing. I battle stress and worry. But I know from where peace comes, and I can find it. I can find clarity during chaos. I can relax, breathe, and find a place of tranquility.

This is a challenge I will face many times, but each time I become stronger, better finding this place of serenity, this place of peace. It is a test for my mind, which can only strengthen me and make me stronger as I prepare for the birth of my baby.

I know where to go.

I can find peace in the storm.

PSALM 4:8

"In peace I will lie down and sleep for you alone, Lord make me dwell in safety."

Notes:_____

_____

_____

_____

_____

_____

_____

_____

_____

_____

_____

_____

_____

_____

_____

_____

_____

_____

_____

_____

_____

_____

_____

_____

_____

_____

FOURTEEN

My Body Is Strong

My body is stronger than even I ever knew. My body is more capable than I've ever expected. Each day I am amazed at how much my body can handle.

This makes me understand just how strong I am to give birth, to labor, to contract, and to deliver my sweet baby. I feel tired and weak at times, but that does not detract from the strength my body possesses to bring this miracle to fruition.

The strength of my body shifts and changes with the growth of my baby. When I go into labor, the strength of my body will shift to birth my child. When my baby is born, the strength of my body will shift to nurture and to provide care.

The strength of my body is amazing, and ever changing to fit the needs of my child. This strength is God-given, a gift and a testament to the miracle of life.

My body is strong

PSALM 18:32

"It is God that girdeth me with strength, and maketh my way perfect."

Notes:_____
_____
_____
_____
_____
_____
_____
_____
_____
_____
_____
_____
_____
_____
_____
_____
_____
_____
_____
_____
_____
_____
_____
_____

FIFTEEN

My Baby Is Mine

My baby is a gift. My baby belongs to me, is my responsibility to care for and nurture. This begins as soon as my baby begins growing in my body. This precious child has been entrusted to me. I am capable of growing and raising this baby.

Knowing this places the responsibility of my baby's well-being in my hands. I can choose the paths that are best for my little one. Because my mind is tune and my body is strong, I can learn and grow into this responsibility.

I may feel afraid at times, but I know where to go for strength and encouragement. My baby will have the best of me.

My baby is mine.

PSALM 127:3

"Lo, children are an heritage of the Lord: and the fruit of the womb is his reward."

Notes:_____
_____
_____
_____
_____
_____
_____
_____
_____
_____
_____
_____
_____
_____
_____
_____
_____
_____
_____
_____
_____
_____
_____
_____

SIXTEEN

I Am Not Afraid of Change

I know that change is part of pregnancy and childbearing. I am not afraid of this. I may battle stress and some worry, but I will overcome this to embrace the changes that come with each new day.

I will focus on the understanding that with change comes growth. This is preparing me, strengthening me for the day I bring my baby into the world, and for the future that lies ahead, when I will raise my child.

I am not afraid of change.

DEUTERONOMY 31:5

*"Be strong and of a good courage,
fear not, nor be afraid of them:
for the Lord thy God, he it is that
doth go with thee; he will not
fail thee, nor forsake thee."*

Notes:_____

_____

_____

_____

_____

_____

_____

_____

_____

_____

_____

_____

_____

_____

_____

_____

_____

_____

_____

_____

_____

SEVENTEEN

I Can Protect My Baby

Because I am in tune with my baby, because I am strong, because I can adapt to change, I am well able to protect my baby. I have the ability to make decisions during my pregnancy that are for the benefit of my child.

The instinct to protect is natural and God-given. It is innate and I don't have to struggle to feel protective. Even when I am not at my best, my baby's wellbeing is my first thought. This is why I am already a powerful mother.

I will protect my baby.

ISAIAH 41:10

"Fear thou not; for I am with thee: be not dismayed; for I am thy God: I will strengthen thee; yea, I will help thee; yea, I will uphold thee with the right hand of my righteousness."

Notes:_____

_____

_____

_____

_____

_____

_____

_____

_____

_____

_____

_____

_____

_____

_____

_____

_____

_____

_____

_____

_____

_____

_____

_____

EIGHTEEN

My Spirit Is Strong

I have strength in my spirit to be pregnant. I have strength in my spirit to labor. I have strength in my spirit to give birth. I have strength in my spirit to be a mother.

I may not always feel full and able, but I know where to go for strength. Because I have strength in my spirit, I can have confidence and I can believe in my ability to have this child.

I have strength of spirit.

PSALM 46:1

"God is our refuge and strength, a very present help in trouble."

Notes:_____

_____

_____

_____

_____

_____

_____

_____

_____

_____

_____

_____

_____

_____

_____

_____

_____

_____

_____

_____

_____

_____

_____

_____

_____

NINETEEN

I Love My Journey

I know that not every part of my pregnancy journey is pleasant. I know this and I love my journey even more. I love that I am learning to grow and adapt. I love that I am becoming stronger, able to endure, and I love that I get to watch this miracle take place in my body.

I love that my tummy is holding a baby inside. I love that I am responsible for my baby's growth and development. I love that soon I will be the one to bring my baby into the world and hold them in my arms. I love that I am becoming a mother.

I love my pregnancy journey.

PSALM 16:11

"Thou wilt shew me the path of life: in thy presence is fulness of joy; at thy right hand there are pleasures for evermore."

Notes:_____

_____

_____

_____

_____

_____

_____

_____

_____

_____

_____

_____

_____

_____

_____

_____

_____

_____

_____

_____

_____

_____

_____

_____

TWENTY

My Body Is Beautiful

The changes in my body are nothing short of miraculous. My body is created in His image, full of immeasurable capability. My body is beautiful. My body is a masterpiece, a work of art by a perfect Artist.

The changes that I see only add to the story that my body tells. The rest of the world may have a standard on what makes a body beautiful, but I have a strong mind. I do not adhere to what the rest of the world thinks. Instead, I have confidence that my body is beautiful and doing something miraculous.

My body is beautiful because it is focused on someone else—the sweet life I'm carrying. I will do the same and focus on my body's purpose. I will not allow this harsh world to steal away the sacred purpose that my body is fulfilling and tear away my confidence. My body is acceptable, miraculous and created with love.

My body is beautiful.

EPHESIANS 2:10

"For we are his workmanship, created in Christ Jesus unto good works, which God hath before ordained that we should walk in them."

Notes:_____

_____

_____

_____

_____

_____

_____

_____

_____

_____

_____

_____

_____

_____

_____

_____

_____

_____

_____

_____

_____

_____

_____

_____

TWENTY-ONE

I Can Have Peace Instead of Fear

I am not afraid. I am not afraid. I am not afraid. Pregnancy is new, a journey that has many turns I cannot understand until I'm amid the experience. I accept that this can sometimes threaten my sense of peace. I understand that I'm a human-being and can succumb to my fears.

But I also know that I do not have to allow fear to take over. I can fight fear and find peace instead. I can turn to the Prince of Peace, and I can conquer fear.

I am learning to not be afraid.

ISAIAH 9:6

"For unto us a child is born, unto us a son is given: and the government shall be upon his shoulder: and his name shall be called Wonderful, Counsellor, The mighty God, The everlasting Father, The Prince of Peace."

Notes:_____

_____

_____

_____

_____

_____

_____

_____

_____

_____

_____

_____

_____

_____

_____

_____

_____

_____

_____

_____

_____

_____

_____

_____

TWENTY-TWO

I Am Not Afraid To Make My Own Decisions

I feel courage to make decisions for myself. I am the one who is carrying my baby. I feel my baby like one else, I understand my baby like no one else, and I know my own body like no one else.

When it comes to making decisions for my baby, I know that I am the most capable because I am my baby's mother. When it comes to deciding what's best, I know I have the instinct and the courage to make the right choice.

I have courage to make choices for my baby.

PSALM 31:24

"Be of good courage, and he shall strengthen your heart, all ye that hope in the Lord."

Notes:_____

_____

_____

_____

_____

_____

_____

_____

_____

_____

_____

_____

_____

_____

_____

_____

_____

_____

_____

_____

_____

_____

_____

_____

_____

TWENTY-THREE

I Am Strong Enough To Make Plans

I have courage. I can make plans for my pregnancy, for my labor and childbirth. I can make plans for my baby with happiness and confidence. I can look forward to the future. I don't have to worry about what may come, for I have peace and I have hope that God holds my future.

Because of this, I can make plans and look forward to tomorrow. Even though I know there is pain in childbearing, I find strength when I plan for the day my baby will arrive. That is what already makes me a wonderful mother.

I am strong enough to plan for tomorrow.

PHILIPPIANS 1:6

"Being confident of this very thing, that he which hath begun a good work in you will perform it until the day of Jesus Christ."

Notes:_____

_____

_____

_____

_____

_____

_____

_____

_____

_____

_____

_____

_____

_____

_____

_____

_____

_____

_____

_____

_____

_____

_____

_____

_____

TWENTY-FOUR

My Mind Is In Tune With God

I am amazed at how much a spiritual connection I am drawn to during my pregnancy. I find comfort that God holds my future. I find comfort in His peace. I place my thoughts in his hands and allow my mind to become in tune with Him.

Through this, I find strength and clarity. I feel strong and capable and even more connected with my baby. This connection defeats my fears and helps me find a place of mental rest. I am learning that if I seek him and draw near through prayer and His Word, I will receive strength and courage.

My mind is in tune with God.

PSALM 145:18

"The Lord is nigh unto all them that call upon him, to all that call upon him in truth."

Notes:_____

_____

_____

_____

_____

_____

_____

_____

_____

_____

_____

_____

_____

_____

_____

_____

_____

_____

_____

_____

_____

_____

_____

_____

_____

TWENTY-FIVE

I Am Not Afraid Of Becoming A Mother

I am excited about the future. I feel confident, capable, and adaptable. I will not be perfect. There is no way I can prepare for everything. But I know that I am equipped with everything I need for the next chapter in my life. I have love, trust, and determination.

There is so much I don't know. But this doesn't have to make me afraid. Instead, I choose to view it as a new opportunity. I will do my best to raise my child and bring them up in the way they should go. I have faith that I can turn to God and He will direct my steps.

I am not afraid of becoming a mother.

JOSHUA 1:9

"Have not I commanded thee? Be strong and of a good courage; be not afraid, neither be thou dismayed: for the Lord thy God is with thee whithersoever thou goest."

Notes:_____

_____

_____

_____

_____

_____

_____

_____

_____

_____

_____

_____

_____

_____

_____

_____

_____

_____

_____

_____

_____

_____

_____

_____

_____

TWENTY-SIX

My Body Can Persevere

My body is strong and capable, even when challenges arise. Not everything may go according to plan, but my body can rise to the occasion. As I grow and change, I can feel things that aren't always easy. I sometimes ache and I know there can be difficulties because of the changes.

Through all of this, I am determined, and I believe in the capability of my body. I don't have to allow these challenges to take over, and I don't have to give in to them. I am strong enough to face them and persevere to the birth experience I desire—and I will fight for it.

My body can persevere.

1 CHRONICLES 16:11

*"Seek the Lord and his strength,
seek his face continually."*

Notes:_____
_____
_____
_____
_____
_____
_____
_____
_____
_____
_____
_____
_____
_____
_____
_____
_____
_____
_____
_____
_____
_____
_____
_____

TWENTY-SEVEN

My Mind Is Strong Enough To Stand By My Decisions

I have a strong body, and I have a strong mind. I can feel confident and assured in the decisions I make, because I am certain they are for the good of my baby and my own wellbeing. I know how to ask questions and search for the answers I need to help me make my decisions.

There may be a lot of pressure to do things a certain way, and others may make me uncomfortable, but I will ultimately make decisions based on my own mind. I am confident, and I will stand by my decisions. They come from certainty within, not from outside influences.

I am strong enough to stand by my decisions.

1 CORINTHIANS 15:58

*"Therefore, my beloved brethren,
be ye stedfast, unmoveable, always
abounding in the work of the Lord,
forasmuch as ye know that your
labour is not in vain in the Lord."*

Notes:_____

_____

_____

_____

_____

_____

_____

_____

_____

_____

_____

_____

_____

_____

_____

_____

_____

_____

_____

_____

_____

_____

_____

TWENTY-EIGHT

I Am Strong Enough To Sacrifice For My Baby

The love I have for my baby is overwhelming and powerful. My entire body and mind are focused on protecting and nourishing my baby. Because of this love, I can sacrifice my own comforts for the good of my little one. I am already learning this skill, and it will remain with me throughout the rest of our lives.

From the moment I conceived, my body was aware and making changes for my baby. As my child grows, I am constantly sacrificing and giving of myself. It is out of love, and I am happy to do it, even if I may be uncomfortable. This is what makes me an amazing, powerful mother.

I am strong enough to sacrifice for my baby.

1 JOHN 3:16

"Hereby perceive we the love of God, because he laid down his life for us: and we ought to lay down our lives for the brethren."

Notes:_____

_____

_____

_____

_____

_____

_____

_____

_____

_____

_____

_____

_____

_____

_____

_____

_____

_____

_____

_____

_____

_____

_____

_____

TWENTY-NINE

I Can Have Peace Even When
I Feel Pressure

There are so many opinions about pregnancy, and many have their own ideas. I feel pressure many times from others who strongly encourage me to conform to their ideas. But I have peace that when I make my decisions, they are for the good of my baby and they are solid.

I don't need to react in anger, but in love and confidence. I don't have to give in to the pressures, but I can stand in the midst of the storm and carry on, for I have the wellbeing of my baby in my every thought.

When the ideas and pressures of others are swirling around me, I will hold fast to peace, and I will quietly carry on.

I have peace even during pressure.

2 THESSALONIANS 3:16

*"Now the Lord of peace himself
give you peace always by all means.
The Lord be with you all."*

Notes:_____

_____

_____

_____

_____

_____

_____

_____

_____

_____

_____

_____

_____

_____

_____

_____

_____

_____

_____

_____

_____

_____

_____

_____

THIRTY

I Am Excited About My Pregnancy

I am thankful for this beautiful opportunity to be pregnant. I am excited about this pregnancy. Not everything about pregnancy is enjoyable or pleasant, but that does not take away the excitement and appreciation I feel for it.

To think that in just a short matter of time I will be holding the baby I am carrying is precious and wonderful. This is the only season in which I will carry this baby in this way. Each day is one-of-a-kind and will pass away into memories. I am determined to find the good in each day, and to remain happy and excited.

I am excited about my pregnancy.

GENESIS 30:13

"And Leah said, Happy am I, for the daughters will call me blessed: and she called his name Asher."

Notes:_____

_____

_____

_____

_____

_____

_____

_____

_____

_____

_____

_____

_____

_____

_____

_____

_____

_____

_____

_____

_____

_____

_____

THIRTY-ONE

I Trust God Through My Pregnancy

My excitement and my happiness is made greater because I trust the Lord through my pregnancy. I cannot completely understand every tiny detail about what is taking place, but I feel assured and at rest because I trust the Lord and I am His creation. He created me, and He knows more about my pregnancy than anyone else on this earth.

My trust is strong, and I can look to His word for affirmation and confidence.

I trust God through my pregnancy.

PSALM 9:10

*"And they that know thy name
will put their trust in thee: for
thou, Lord, hast not forsaken
them that seek thee."*

Notes:_____

_____

_____

_____

_____

_____

_____

_____

_____

_____

_____

_____

_____

_____

_____

_____

_____

_____

_____

_____

_____

_____

_____

_____

THIRTY-TWO

My Baby Is Already Fearfully
& Wonderfully Made

Each day brings new developments and changes for my baby. The growth of my baby is incredible and miraculous. God has His hand on my baby, for my baby is His creation, beautifully and perfectly made.

I sometimes have doubts and fears about my baby, but I am assured by knowing that my baby is in God's hands. I do my best each day, and I find peace and comfort in God's Word. The remarkable beauty of life growing inside me never ceases to amaze me. It brings me fresh gratitude each day.

My baby is fearfully and wonderfully made.

PSALM 139:13

"For thou hast possessed my reins: thou hast covered me in my mother's womb."

Notes:_____

_____

_____

_____

_____

_____

_____

_____

_____

_____

_____

_____

_____

_____

_____

_____

_____

_____

_____

_____

_____

_____

_____

_____

THIRTY-THREE

I Am Not Afraid Of My Doctor

I am not afraid of the doctor who is handling my pregnancy. My doctor is the professional I have chosen to coach and to guide me. I have done my best in establishing a good relationship, asked good questions, and have made my best effort. I understand that no matter my doctor's manner, I am ultimately the one who gets to make the decisions.

This confidence lets me know there is no reason to fear the doctor. I am not afraid. I also know I can turn to the Great Physician in prayer if I need help and strength. I find courage in this, and I have the confidence I need to make strong decisions and feel comfortable with them.

I am not afraid of the doctor.

HEBREWS 4:16

"Let us therefore come boldly unto the throne of grace, that we may obtain mercy, and find grace to help in time of need."

Notes:_____

_____

_____

_____

_____

_____

_____

_____

_____

_____

_____

_____

_____

_____

_____

_____

_____

_____

_____

_____

_____

_____

_____

_____

_____

THIRTY-FOUR

I Trust My Spouse

I trust my spouse during my pregnancy. I know it can be a challenge to remain a team at certain times, especially when I don't feel well and I don't know how to share my thoughts and feelings. I trust the one whom my soul loves to stand by me during this season.

We chose one another and are committed to one another. Our love and our trust will stand firm through the tests that pregnancy may bring. I trust my spouse to support and uphold me, and because of that I have peace and don't feel alone. It makes me excited to start the next chapter with him.

I trust my spouse.

SONG OF SOLOMON 8:7

"Many waters cannot quench love, neither can the floods drown it: if a man would give all the substance of his house for love, it would utterly be contemned."

Notes:_____

_____
_____
_____
_____
_____
_____
_____
_____
_____
_____
_____
_____
_____
_____
_____
_____
_____
_____
_____
_____
_____
_____

THIRTY-FIVE

I Lovingly Accept The Physical Changes In My Body

I am growing and changing every day. It is tempting to become dissatisfied with what I see if I allow my perspective to be influenced. When I look at my body, I see a capable body that is holding new life. When I look at my body, I see strength and adaptability.

My perspective of my body is based on what my body is accomplishing, not on how it is perceived by others. This focus makes me proud of what I am able to do instead of ashamed or inferior. My body is doing incredible things, and I am amazing.

I accept the changes in my body.

EPHESIANS 5:29

"For no man ever yet hated his own flesh; but nourisheth and cherisheth it, even as the Lord the church:"

Notes:_____

_____
_____
_____
_____
_____
_____
_____
_____
_____
_____
_____
_____
_____
_____
_____
_____
_____
_____
_____
_____

LABOR, DELIVERY & MOTHERHOOD

THIRTY-SIX

My Body Can Labor On Its Own

My body is fully capable to labor on its own. Even though I may not understand every tiny detail of labor, my body instinctively knows what to do. I trust my body, and I will follow the natural path my body takes, without fear.

I am focused. I am determined. I appreciate those that will stand with me during my labor, but I ultimately will be taking this journey, and I have confidence in my body to labor courageously.

I am strong enough to labor on my own.

PROVERBS 31:17

*"She girdeth her loins with strength,
and strengtheneth her arms."*

Notes:_____
_____
_____
_____
_____
_____
_____
_____
_____
_____
_____
_____
_____
_____
_____
_____
_____
_____
_____
_____
_____
_____
_____
_____
_____

THIRTY-SEVEN

I Am Stronger Than My Pain

I can bear the pain of labor because I am stronger than my contractions. I am stronger than the pain. I am stronger than self-doubt. I can defeat my fears and I can breathe through my labor. I am strong enough to persevere. I am strong enough to press on, and I am strong enough to get to the end of this, where I am holding my baby in my arms.

I've spent my pregnancy growing stronger. I've been strengthened through the growth of my pregnancy, through time and through challenges.

I am stronger than my pain.

PROVERBS 18:10

"The name of the Lord is a strong tower: the righteous runneth into it, and is safe."

Notes:_____

_____
_____
_____
_____
_____
_____
_____
_____
_____
_____
_____
_____
_____
_____
_____
_____
_____
_____
_____
_____
_____
_____

THIRTY-EIGHT

I Am Not Afraid Of Pain

I am not afraid of the pain of labor. I know it will come, and I am ready for it. I have conditioned and prepared my mind, and I am able to view the pain of labor as a positive thing.

Labor pain does not mean something is wrong. In fact, the pain of contractions is a good thing, because it means my body is working and preparing for my baby. The pain of each contraction is my body functioning perfectly, just as it should. This gives me reassurance and strength to breathe through each contraction.

I am not afraid of pain.

PSALM 22:19

*"But be not thou far from me,
O Lord: O my strength, haste
thee to help me."*

Notes:_____

_____

_____

_____

_____

_____

_____

_____

_____

_____

_____

_____

_____

_____

_____

_____

_____

_____

_____

_____

_____

_____

THIRTY-NINE

I Can Breathe Through This

Each contraction that I feel means that I am that much closer to my baby. I can breathe... breathe in... breathe out... I can feel my body working as I get closer and closer to meeting my baby.

Each contraction is a mountain. It rises, peaks, and then falls. I can breathe to that peak. I can get over that peak, and I can move on from it.

I can breathe through this.

PSALM 18:2

"The Lord is my rock, and my fortress, and my deliverer; my God, my strength, in whom I will trust; my buckler, and the horn of my salvation, and my high tower."

Notes:_____

_____
_____
_____
_____
_____
_____
_____
_____
_____
_____
_____
_____
_____
_____
_____
_____
_____
_____
_____
_____
_____

FORTY

The Pain Will Not Last Forever

These contractions that I am feeling are only temporary. This contraction will not last. It will fade. And so will the next. I can breathe through this contraction. It will fade away. I can breathe through it. My labor is progressing, and I am gleaning strength from the vision of my baby in my arms.

Soon... very soon, I will be holding my baby.

This will not last. It is only a minute. And then it passes. I can endure for a minute. One more minute. I can endure for one more minute. I know where my help comes from. I can endure.

The pain will not last. I can endure.

PSALM 121:1-2

"I will lift up mine eyes unto the hills, from whence cometh my help. My help cometh from the Lord, which made heaven and earth."

Notes:_____

_____

_____

_____

_____

_____

_____

_____

_____

_____

_____

_____

_____

_____

_____

_____

_____

_____

_____

_____

_____

_____

_____

_____

_____

FORTY-ONE

The Love I Feel For My Baby Helps Me Push Through

I love my child. I will soon be holding my baby. The love I feel is overwhelming, even in the midst of contractions. The thought of holding my baby gives me the strength to endure through these contractions.

I have so much love for my child, I am willing to endure, and I will endure courageously. My body knows what to do. My mind is tuned in to my baby and tuned in to my body.

My love is powerful. It helps me fight fear and relax into my labor. I am feeling the rhythm of my labor and I am getting closer and closer to embracing my precious baby.

My love gives me strength and endurance.

JOHN 15:9

"As the Father hath loved me, so have I loved you: continue ye in my love."

Notes:_____

_____

_____

_____

_____

_____

_____

_____

_____

_____

_____

_____

_____

_____

_____

_____

_____

_____

_____

_____

_____

_____

_____

_____

_____

_____

FORTY-TWO

I Can Focus Through The Pain

As my body contracts, I can breathe. I keep breathing. I keep focusing. I focus on getting to the next second, the next minute, the next phase. My mind is focused on the goal—my baby. I will hold my baby soon. My labor has beautiful purpose.

I focus on my strength. I have strength beyond belief. I focus on my determination. I am determined to the core. I focus on getting through this minute. I can and I will breathe through this minute.

And I focus on my overwhelming love.

I can stay focused.

PROVERBS 4:25

*"Let thine eyes look right on,
and let thine eyelids look
straight before thee."*

Notes:_____

_____
_____
_____
_____
_____
_____
_____
_____
_____
_____
_____
_____
_____
_____
_____
_____
_____
_____
_____
_____
_____
_____
_____
_____

FORTY-THREE

My Body Is Amazing

It hurts, but it's supposed to hurt. It's tightening, because it's supposed to contract. I'm in the midst of this challenge, but my body is naturally following a rhythm of labor. It is working for me, working for my baby. It's amazing! My body is doing what it needs to do, all on its own.

I am reminded of how incredible I am, of all the incredible things I can do. I can have this baby. I will have this baby.

My body is amazing.

ISAIAH 40:29

*"He giveth power to the faint;
and to them that have no might
he increaseth strength."*

Notes:_____

_____

_____

_____

_____

_____

_____

_____

_____

_____

_____

_____

_____

_____

_____

_____

_____

_____

_____

_____

_____

_____

_____

_____

_____

FORTY-FOUR

I Can Have Joy Through My Labor

I am not afraid. I have control over my anxieties and my worries. I defeated them long ago. Now there is room for excitement and joy, even as I labor. The very thought that I am here, right now, brings incredible joy. My baby is arriving!

Each breath, each second, brings me closer to that meeting. The joy is incredible. It is strengthening me and helps me stay determined and focused. It brings a happy feeling to my surroundings, and everything is tinged with an air of excitement.

I am joyous in my labor.

NEHEMIAH 8:10

"…for this day is holy unto our Lord: neither be ye sorry; for the joy of the Lord is your strength."

Notes:_____
_____
_____
_____
_____
_____
_____
_____
_____
_____
_____
_____
_____
_____
_____
_____
_____
_____
_____
_____
_____
_____
_____

FORTY-FIVE

I Am Unstoppable

I have made it to this point. I have faced and conquered challenges. I have faced and conquered fear. I have persevered through hardships and changes. Now I'm here, laboring and preparing to meet my baby.

I am unstoppable! I can do this! I can bring this baby into the world, I can care for this baby, and I can be an unstoppable mother. I've already proven that I can do whatever I need to do for the sake of my wellbeing and my baby's wellbeing. The journey is just beginning, and I'm ready.

I am unstoppable!

PHILIPPIANS 4:13

"I can do all things through Christ which strengtheneth me."

Notes:_____

_____

_____

_____

_____

_____

_____

_____

_____

_____

_____

_____

_____

_____

_____

_____

_____

_____

_____

_____

_____

_____

_____

_____

_____

_____

FORTY-SIX

I Am A Capable Mother

I know I am a capable mother. I've already proven that I am, I've already taken the steps to protect and nurture my baby. I have stayed focused on my baby, aware of my baby, tuned in to my baby. I am connected in a way that no other human being can be connected.

I have what it takes to be what my child needs. I can care for, provide for and protect my baby from now on. I have the love, the determination, and the strength required—I've shown it over these past nine months.

I am already a capable mother.

PROVERBS 31:15

*"She riseth also while it is yet night,
and giveth meat to her household,
and a portion to her maidens."*

Notes:_____
_____
_____
_____
_____
_____
_____
_____
_____
_____
_____
_____
_____
_____
_____
_____
_____
_____
_____
_____
_____
_____
_____
_____

FORTY-SEVEN

I Will Be An Encouraging Mother

I understand what it is like to face hardships. I know what it's like to feel discouraged. I've travelled that road on my own. Because I understand that, I will be an encouraging mother to my child. I will be there for my child when they fall, when they feel discouraged or inadequate. I will be the voice that reassures them that they can get up and try again, because I have had to get up and try again.

My pregnancy, my labor, my birth experience has allowed me to feel weariness and pain. It has given me the ability to know there is always more, and to share that encouragement with my child. I have something very special I can share with them.

I will be an encouraging mother.

1 THESSALONIANS 5:11

"Wherefore comfort yourselves together, and edify one another, even as also ye do."

Notes:_____

_____
_____
_____
_____
_____
_____
_____
_____
_____
_____
_____
_____
_____
_____
_____
_____
_____
_____
_____
_____
_____
_____
_____

FORTY-EIGHT

I Will Be A Firm Mother

My pregnancy has taught me that I must gather myself up in strength when challenges arise. It has taught me that I cannot hide away from all the difficulties I face. I have learned to have grit, to face my fears, and to become stronger in spite of the hardships I face.

I will pass this down to my child. I know my child will face challenges in life, but because of my own challenges I will be able help my child find strength. I now have the ability to teach my child to be strong, to stand firm, and to face challenges and be made better by them.

I will be a firm mother.

PHILIPPIANS 4:1

"Therefore, my brethren dearly beloved and longed for, my joy and crown, so stand fast in the Lord, my dearly beloved."

Notes:_____

_____

_____

_____

_____

_____

_____

_____

_____

_____

_____

_____

_____

_____

_____

_____

_____

_____

_____

_____

_____

FORTY-NINE

I Will Be An Instinctive Mother

I am deeply connected with my child. It started during my pregnancy and has become stronger with time. I am instinctively aware of my child. This connection is beautiful and allows me insight to my child's needs in a way that no one else will be able to understand.

I will forever be tuned in to my child. It will never fade. It will always give me courage and assurance as my child grows.

I am an instinctive mother.

PROVERBS 22:6

"Train up a child in the way he should go: and when he is old, he will not depart from it."

Notes:_____

_____

_____

_____

_____

_____

_____

_____

_____

_____

_____

_____

_____

_____

_____

_____

_____

_____

_____

_____

_____

_____

_____

_____

FIFTY

I Will Be A Loving Mother

There is no love like a mother's love. I understand this. I have felt this every day of my pregnancy. A mother's love is powerful. A mother's love is protective. A mother's love is selfless. I have already lived this.

The overwhelming love I have for my baby will help me to be the guiding steps they watch, the encouragement and affirmation they crave, and the firm hand they need. My child can feel it. I can feel it. It binds us together and is source of all I do for my child, whether in correction or approval. It will help me raise my child to become a healthy, strong adult.

I have learned how to conquer fears through love, because God's perfect love casts out all fear. I know where to turn. I know where to go. I know how to love.

I am fearless.

PROVERBS 31:25-30

"Strength and honour are her clothing; and she shall rejoice in time to come. She openeth her mouth with wisdom; and in her tongue is the law of kindness. She looketh well to the ways of her household, and eateth not the bread of idleness. Her children arise up, and call her blessed; her husband also, and he praiseth her. Many daughters have done virtuously, but thou excellest them all. Favour is deceitful, and beauty is vain: but a woman that feareth the Lord, she shall be praised."

Notes:_____

_____

_____

_____

_____

_____

_____

_____

_____

_____

_____

_____

_____

_____

_____

_____

_____

_____

_____

_____

_____

_____

_____

Notes:_____

_____

_____

_____

_____

_____

_____

_____

_____

_____

_____

_____

_____

_____

_____

_____

_____

_____

_____

_____

_____

_____

_____

_____

Made in the USA
Las Vegas, NV
13 July 2022

51508184R00090